in His words

Besorah Press

in His words
Copyright © 2022 by Helen Bishop
All rights reserved.
No part of this publication
may be reproduced or transmitted,
in any form or any means,
without permission.

First published 2022 by
Besorah Press
Mornington, Victoria, Australia
besorahpress@gmail.com

Except where indicated, all Scripture quotations are taken from the New King James Version. Copyright © 1979, 1980, 1982 by Thomas Nelson, Inc. Used by permission. All rights reserved.

Scripture taken from the Holy Scriptures, Tree of Life Version. Copyright © 2014, 2016 by the Tree of Life Bible Society. Used by permission of the Tree of Life Bible Society.

Scripture taken from the Holy Bible, New International Version. Copyright © 1973, 1978, 1984 by International Bible Society. Used by permission of Zondervan. All rights reserved.

ISBN: 978-0-646-83986-8
Edited by Estelle Clarkson
Cover designed by usagiart design
Front cover: Mount Martha foreshore, Victoria
Back cover: Fossil Beach, Mornington, Victoria

This book is available by contacting: besorahpress@gmail.com

Besorah for the Brokenhearted

¹ *The Ruach of Adonai Elohim is on me, because Adonai has anointed me to proclaim Good News to the poor. He has sent me to bind up the brokenhearted, to proclaim liberty to the captives, and the opening of the prison to those who are bound,*

ISAIAH 61: 1 (TLV)

Thank you for opening this book. Herein you will find a collection of writings and poetry that have come from the Heart of Father God which expresses His love for all His creation. You are invited to write down any thoughts, ideas or drawings you may have on the blank pages within. Accept this invitation to wander at will as you turn the pages and begin your journey…

The Father

I am in the colour of the flowers

the green in the grass

the songs of the birds.

Everything in creation is sacred.

The texture and colour in My garden are woven with My hands.

I change the colours with the seasons, for they are in

a continual cycle of change.

[1] *To everything there is a season,*
A time for every purpose under heaven

ECCLESIASTES 3: 1

Seek and Ye Shall Find...

The Beginning... 1
- Listen 2
- Untitled I 3
- Vested Secrets 4
- That First Heartbeat 5
- Untitled II 7
- The Living Word 9
- Untitled III 11
- The Father's Message to the World 13
- The Cork 14

Hope 19
- Hope 21
- Untitled IV 23
- Disappointments 25
- We Wait 26
- Untitled V 28
- Untitled VI 29
- Untitled VII 30
- Untitled VIII 31

Holiness through Wholeness 33

    Untitled IX 35

    Untitled X 37

    The Son 39

    Untitled XI 41

    Untitled XII 42

    Untitled XIII 43

    Captured 45

    My Peaceful Healing Love 46

    A Season for Everything 49

    The Rock 50

    Value 52

    Untitled XIV 53

    Untitled XV 54

Pathway of Promises 55

    Untitled XVI 56

    Untitled XVII 57

    Untitled XVIII 59

    Untitled XIX 61

    Untitled XX 62

    Untitled XXI 63

    Presents for you 64

    Untitled XXII 65

    Untitled XXIII 67

    Behind Closed Eyes 68

    Untitled XXIV 69

Untitled XXV 70

Untitled XXVI 71

Untitled XXVII 71

The Golden Harvest 73

The Harvest 75

Untitled XXVIII 76

Untitled XXIX 77

The Creative Child 79

Splinters of the Cross 80

Divine Purpose 81

Love Letter to Jesus 83

Ffald y Brenin, Wales I 85

Ffald y Brenin, Wales II 86

Masquerade 87

The Door 89

The Well 91

Untitled XXX 92

Untitled XXXI 93

The Seed 95

Untitled XXXII 97

Untitled XXXIII 98

Untitled XXXIV 99

The Master's Hand 101

In Tune with The Father 102

Untitled XXXV 104

Untitled XXXVI 106

Untitled XXXVII 107
Scribe of Life 109
The Song of the Warrior 111
The Timeless One 112
Acknowledgements 117
About the authors 118

The Beginning...

[8] *But now, O Lord,*
You are our Father;
We are the clay, and You our potter;
And all we are the work of Your hand.

                                                        ISAIAH 64: 8

Listen

I am the silent voice that speaks to your spirit

I pour My healing oil into your aching heart

I answer every question you have asked

I reveal the wonders of the universe to you

Let the music flow through your spirit

Let My Spirit guide your hands and mind

Listen and let your tears of joy flow into the beauty of each note

Wondrous as it draws you into the mystery of how…

My Spirit flows in the music My beloved create

I speak through the words that they write

Even those who know not of Me…yet

For one day they will come to Me

The Lord poured His Praise and worship music into the heart of David, the shepherd boy before he became David, the King of Israel.

Untitled I

The Wind blows the sand in endless drifts

Singing to the air and sky

Each dune is sculpted according to the Wind's desire

The secret lies in the constant shifting

Nothing stays the same

Except The One who owns the Wind.

Vested Secrets

The wind blows in from the shore speaking to whoever will listen
    its speech intonates
        pausing
            in conversation
                asking questions
                    knowing the answers.
        The sea rumbles in the background
      a constant accompaniment to the wind, its master
without it, it is silent
apart from the hiss of bubbles rising up from the sand
              greeting the incoming tide
                  itself a servant to others.
          Wind and sea
        sand and rain
      all-knowing elements of their timeless earth
    when was it born?
how was it created?

    The answers are vested secrets spoken only by the wind.

9 October 2013 - Hayle, Cornwall, England

Vested Secrets was written following two long walks on the beach and clifftops, painting and walking barefoot in the wind and the rain and the incoming tide. When I came back, I thought I could hear people talking or a TV but it was wind howling around the house.

That First Heartbeat

The Father

Remember when your heart first beat?

Remember when you first moved in her womb?

You reached out to Me, knowing I, your Creator, was making you

I spoke to you in your spirit and told you of the love I have for you

My warmth wrapped around you, secure in My embrace

See how you grew with each heartbeat, firstly it was your mother's, then yours as well.

The Child

You held me within, secure, floating

Suddenly I felt her shock, her trauma

Waves of fear, anxiety, grief tried to engulf me

Afloat in Your comfort, I settled finally in Your love.

My birth was a shock

I didn't want to come out and face the world, to be a part of it

I was born into sadness, mixed with joy

I knew I was loved but there was something missing…

If only I could return…

Were you fading from my view? My perception?

I was alone, yet surrounded by those who loved me

I lost sight of You, became deaf to Your voice.

It was only when I had run out of options that I finally turned back to You, my Father.

Did I have to lose my earthly father for that to happen…?

Untitled II

Time rides on the breeze, shifting the sands of history, exposing the enigmas of this world, only to cover an undiscovered answer.

> Time passes
>> the sand shifts
>>> the hidden is uncovered.

A single grain of sand carried far from its origin to be laid to rest at its destination

> – history and destiny –

so far apart yet enjoined into the timeless and unending mystery of Creation.

The Child

You told me You will give me the answers.
I said I didn't have any questions.
You said You will give me the questions to the answers.

[2] *For there is nothing covered that will not be revealed, nor hidden that will not be known.*

LUKE 12: 2

This is the Living Word of God, His scripture, the Bible.

Build on the Rock

[24] "Therefore whoever hears these sayings of Mine, and does them, I will liken him to a wise man who built his house on the rock: [25] and the rain descended, the floods came, and the winds blew and beat on that house; and it did not fall, for it was founded on the rock."

MATTHEW 7: 24-25

The Living Word

Judge not the book

by its cover

peel its cover off

pare its spine away

with care dissect each page

not just from its spine

but within each page

savour each living word.

        Sense

        the essence

        of each word

        each letter

        why it was conceived and joined

        to the next

        and the next

        to the next.

                        Then

                        and only then

                        will you perceive

                        the Truth.

Untitled III

Ephemeral beings impart My Wisdom on those who choose to listen. My Angels watch over all My chosen ones – guarding, protecting and guiding. My essence has been poured over them to be absorbed into their souls and spirits. It is then for them to take it out to the world.

Precious gems of wisdom

Precious words of hope

Precious words of love

11 For He shall give His angels charge over you,
To keep you in all your ways.

PSALM 91: 11

¹² This is My commandment, that you love one another as I have loved you.

JOHN 15: 12

²⁶ Look at the birds of the air, for they neither sow nor reap nor gather into barns; yet your heavenly Father feeds them. Are you not of more value than they?

MATTHEW 6: 26

¹¹ When I was a child, I spoke as a child, I understood as a child, I thought as a child; but when I became a man, I put away childish things. ¹² For now we see in a mirror, dimly, but then face to face. Now I know in part, but then I shall know just as I also am known.

1 CORINTHIANS 13: 11-12

The Father's Message to the World

The energy that makes the atom that makes the blade of grass, to the animal that feeds on it, to the next animal that feeds on that – it is My omnipotent power that creates it all.

I made the earth to be interwoven with all My mysteries, all My wonders for you to behold.

I made the love that binds My people together for that is My gift to you all. Any negative thoughts, emotions, behaviours are not of Me. They clash with **WHO I AM**. They have no place in My world, My people. So, love one another with all your shortcomings – this is My commandment, that you love one another as I have loved you.

From the rays of the sun to the grains of sand on the fathomless ocean floor – know that they were made by My hand. I give the birds their song, I tell them where to nest in the trees I provide. They know Me as I know them. The trees know the life force I give them. I know their being, because I created them from a thought from which a spark of life then created the atom that created the seed from which it grew.

Know that I created this world for all to live in and grow and flourish. Love My nature in Creation as much as I love you.

Man has managed to discover what he thinks is the basis of all life forms. He must come to understand that the energy he has found is My omnipotent power – no other life force has created it. This is the same power that binds the universe, that radiates from the sun, that reflects from the moon.

The universe has no boundaries – there is no edge. It is My sovereignty that governs how the Heavens, the Earth, the Universe and everything in them were created. This is beyond the comprehension of man – it is not for him to know. He may think he knows but he does not and cannot.

Love and respect the world I gave you, with all its inhabitants of My Creation.

The Cork

The Child

Unknown shores

Distant land tantalisingly close

Yet the wind calls me away

A storm rages

Caught in a whirlpool I am pulled down into the depths

Almost touching the bottom…

Cast adrift on a boundless ocean

Vulnerable to all elements

Waves crash down

Dragging me down into a lightless unfathomable depth

Blinded, lost, no identity, self lost

Remorseless power roars

Swirling, eddying in a wilderness

Innate buoyancy kicks in…

Engulfing storm looms overhead

I am caught in a whirlpool

Pulling me down into the depths

Feet almost touching the bottom

Darkness closes in…

    Cast adrift upon a boundless ocean

Subject to all elements

    Vulnerable

Waves crash down and pitch me up into the wind

Only to be dragged down by the remorseless current.

Innate buoyancy pushes me skywards to burst into the air…

Cast adrift on a boundless ocean

    Vulnerable to all elements

Waves crash down

Current grasps hold, dragging down into lightless depths

    identity lost

    blinded

Released - innate inner buoyancy takes hold

　　　　Escape into, shooting upwards towards light blue

　　　　　　　　　　Bursting into air

　　　　　　　　　　　Gasping

Startled by an unknown touch

　　　　I cry out for life

A hand reaches for mine

　　　　Pulling me upwards

Releasing me into the light

　　　　　　Innate inner buoyancy kicks in

I was a cork floating on Your boundless sea

　　　　　　At times waves crashed over me

But I resurfaced each time – pulled up by an innate inner buoyancy

　　　　　　By the inner will to survive.

Currents steered me in all directions

Until one day amidst a storm

When I thought I was finally drowning

I was washed onto a deserted island

I thought I was alone but I was not

For You were there to greet me as I was washed up on the shore

The Saviour, Jesus Christ

Plunge into the depths

Have no fear

For I will be with you

To reveal the mysteries, the Truth.

The shadow of My empty cross

Tells the story of part of My mortal life

I came to teach of peace and love

Knowing that some would reject Me.

Even as a boy I knew how My future life on earth would unfold. To know that is the ultimate Truth. It is written for all to see, far more will be revealed if only they would seek the Truth.

The Father sent Me to fulfill the Truth.

Hope

The Child

SHE was lost in a fog...

Her spirit said "Wait! ... I can hear His whisper.

Come this way".

Jesus our Lord is Hope personified and faith in Him brings our Hope into fruition.

Hope

Hope barely existed in Despair's icy snow

chilled to its core Hope lay there undisturbed

until one day Winter's wind gathered Hope up

in an almighty gale colliding with the highest mountain

sweeping Hope up through pregnant clouds

towards a sun whose rays wrapped Hope in a blanket of warmth

    melting Hope

        transforming Hope

            into a longed-for droplet

                falling towards a parched earth

            where Hope spread and multiplied

        into a stream of living water

    quenching the desert

bringing growth

    green shoots

        reaching for the mountain

            reaching for the sky

                reaching for The Son.

As the Lord envelopes your life darkness leaves, light encompasses you and freedom comes.

*17 Until the day breaks
And the shadows flee away...*

SONG OF SOLOMON 2: 17A

Untitled IV

She blinks……

How is she to see past the pain and hurt that she sees in the world?

She blinks……

Her past reflects in her eyes and the shadows deepen. Is there any hope or will she always see pain?

She blinks……

Is there someone out there that can get past her walls and touch the place where pain dwells, where she waits and watches?

She blinks……

Then He comes……

She blinks again……

Is what she is seeing real?

She blinks……

He is still there and is holding the hope. He will not leave her!
He will not judge her! He said He died for her. He went to the cross just for her!

She blinks……

The shadows are going, and the light has come into her eyes.
The pain that resided for so long has been replaced with His love.

She blinks……

And He is there……Always.

⁴ *Love suffers long and is kind; love does not envy; love does not parade itself, is not puffed up;* ⁵ *does not behave rudely, does not seek its own, is not provoked, thinks no evil;* ⁶ *does not rejoice in iniquity, but rejoices in the truth;* ⁷ *bears all things, believes all things, hopes all things, endures all things.*
¹³ *And now abide faith, hope, love, these three; but the greatest of these is love.*

1 Corinthians 13: 4-7, 13

Disappointments

They come when you don't expect them.
Daily, weekly, monthly, yearly, never stopping, never ending.
Life is going well and you're happy but then they come again…
disappointments.

You make decisions that are joyful, you laugh.
Then they are snatched away just like that.
We think that we are alone in this, but we are not.
How can others help when really, we are all riding the same wave?

People come into your life and make it richer, more beautiful but the disappointments are always there.
Then something happens and there is a change.
What is it or who is it that suddenly shines Hope into the disappointment?
It is the One, it is Him.

One of the beautiful people He has brought into your life shows you the way to Him.
You don't know Him yet, but you will.
You will go on a journey and get to know the One who will take away the disappointments and replace them with Hope.

You will get to know the One who loves you so much that He suffered, who went to the cross and died for you.
Life is still messy, and disappointments are still there but now the One who bore it all for you replaces them with Hope.
A Hope so real and tangible you can taste it.

We Wait

We wait with wonder and joyful expectation for our child to be born. Family, friends and community also wait with excitement to see this beautiful new life.

It will not be long now…

Then tragedy strikes

The bottom falls out of my world
Pain in my heart, it's ripped in two
There is a big piece missing from it
The place my child was filling and would continue to fill is gone
My feelings are now raw like a knife's edge
Pain so consuming
How to process this I do not know
Life skills I don't have for this
Pain so consuming
Numbness, why and how
Pain on family and friends' faces, so hard to see and all because of our loss.

Life continues all around me, oblivious of my pain, the world keeps moving but no-one sees.
Years just continue on but the pain stays
The journey is hard.

There is a very small glimmer of light a long way off
It's offered to me but I don't see it yet.
The journey continues, many years pass and I'm still in pain, behind the mask.

I have an encounter with the source of the glimmer of light
I hide my hurt as I don't want others to see
But the source sees...
The grief weighs me down
Is there really a chance to be free of it?
The glimmer of light grows a bit bigger but only highlights the brokenness inside.

Can I be repaired? Healed of this?
The light goes into the brokenness and starts to remove the despair and grief. Slowly, gently and with such loving tenderness.
Tenderness so indescribable, so beautiful, slowly repairs my heart.
The journey continues as it's a slow process and needs to be done with care. The source is in no hurry.
While the source repairs me, heals me, a relationship develops.
I then get to know the source of my hope and healing – Jesus!
I am now whole again.
Jesus has filled the hole in my heart.
Wow what does the future hold?
I do not know but I am excited and full of hope.

Untitled V

When you were drowning whose Hand did you grasp as you took what you thought was your last breath?

As you stood on the precipice waiting for the decision to be made who stood in front of you to gently guide you back to live another day?

Who kissed your tears away as you sobbed your heart out thinking there was no release from your trap?

Who held you as you travelled through those nightmares and led you to the door to escape?

Who delivered you from evil as you confronted your terrors?

Jesus, my Saviour

14 But Jesus said, "Let the little children come to Me, and do not forbid them; for of such is the kingdom of heaven."

MATTHEW 19: 14

1 But now, thus says the Lord, who created you, O Jacob,
And He who formed you, O Israel:
"Fear not, for I have redeemed you;
I have called you by your name;
You are Mine.
2 When you pass through the waters, I will be with you;
And through the rivers, they shall not overflow you.
When you walk through the fire, you shall not be burned,
Nor shall the flame scorch you.
3 For I am the Lord your God,
The Holy One of Israel, your Savior;

ISAIAH 43: 1 – 3A

Untitled VI

She came to her eternal Father defeated.

Born a perfect baby on the outside

inwardly her spirit and soul were scarred by the history that came before her.

Her soul was laid bare, wounded and weeping.

No-one could give her the answers she needed to hold close to her –

the promises of what was to come that deep down her soul knew

had to be there, knew where they lay hidden.

Only her spirit knew of the Hope that awaited her.

A Prayer of Repentance

¹ Have mercy upon me, O God,
According to Your lovingkindness;
According to the multitude of Your tender mercies,
Blot out my transgressions.
² Wash me thoroughly from my iniquity,
And cleanse me from my sin.

⁷ Purge me with hyssop, and I shall be clean;
Wash me, and I shall be whiter than snow.

¹⁴ Deliver me from the guilt of bloodshed, O God,
The God of my salvation,
And my tongue shall sing aloud of Your righteousness.
                                                 PSALM 51: 1-2, 7, 14

Untitled VII

You may sleep, but at times you are drawn into parts that lie in the depths of hell – unfathomed in worldly life. This is where your spirit takes your soul to meet Me in this place of darkness.

I AM the Way, the Truth and the Life.

Let Me lead you.

*⁸ If I ascend into heaven, You are there;
If I make my bed in hell, behold, You are there.*

PSALM 139: 8

*⁴ Yea, though I walk through the valley of the shadow of death,
I will fear no evil;
For You are with me;
Your rod and Your staff, they comfort me.*

PSALM 23: 4

Untitled VIII

Father God

There will come a time when you will be taken to somewhere afar.

Remember – your ancestors travelled afar under My guidance.

Infinity runs off the page, off the canvas

Try to catch it if you will – like quicksilver it cannot be contained, only He can hold it in His Hands, it runs from Hand to Hand.

The Child

His cross remains in the soil where it was left to decay. Winds have picked up its remains and taken them far and wide across the globe.

Infinity – can't see the wall – there is none

Infinity has no end

His love has no end

Our spirits live on for eternity

This world, this life is but a capsule in a never-ending existence.

Every sound ever made exists – you only have to listen for them

A bomb explodes…

The last breath of Him…

They both echo on and on…

The Words He spoke are held safely in our hearts

These treasured Words echo in our hearts for eternity

Holiness through Wholeness

While the soul may be hurting, the Holy Spirit is above,
pouring Healing Oil over the wounds.

Untitled IX

Cast off the shell

Shed your old skin

Renewed in an infinite love

Let your spirit bask in the glow of His heart

Renewed in His Spirit, another life takes root.

[17] Therefore, if anyone is in Christ, he is a new creation; old things have passed away; behold, all things have become new.
2 CORINTHIANS 5: 17

⁷ *Where can I go from Your Spirit?*
Or where can I flee from Your presence?
⁸ *If I ascend into heaven, You are there;*
If I make my bed in hell, behold, You are there.
⁹ *If I take the wings of the morning,*
And dwell in the uttermost parts of the sea,
¹⁰ *Even there Your hand shall lead me,*
And Your right hand shall hold me.

PSALM 139: 7-10

¹ *O Lord, our Lord,*
How excellent is Your name in all the earth,
Who have set Your glory above the heavens!
² *Out of the mouth of babes and nursing infants*
You have ordained strength,
Because of Your enemies,
That You may silence the enemy and the avenger.
³ *When I consider Your heavens, the work of Your fingers,*
The moon and the stars, which You have ordained,
⁴ *What is man that You are mindful of him,*
And the son of man that You visit him?
⁵ *For You have made him a little lower than the angels,*
And You have crowned him with glory and honor.
⁶ *You have made him to have dominion over the works of Your hands;*
You have put all things under his feet,
⁷ *All sheep and oxen -*
Even the beasts of the field,
⁸ *The birds of the air,*
And the fish of the sea
That pass through the paths of the seas.
⁹ *O Lord, our Lord,*
How excellent is Your name in all the earth!

PSALM 8

Untitled X

Close out the world

and what do you find?

Where do you go?

Your spirit leads your soul to places unworldly

to see things that you can't describe – from another realm.

So abstract.

In rapturous awe of His Love.

The Son

While the sun casts empty shadows
providing only shade
the Son casts a shadow of light
anointed with love and healing
for whoever chooses to walk in it
leaving their old life behind.

        Daylight will not reveal Him to our eyes
        yet He is everywhere.
        In the dark of night he draws His
        comfort around us.

                Loneliness is an unknown word
                for those who know and love Him.
                To be alone with Him is divine
                to walk with Him is Life.

Seek Him if you will
for you need only ask.
Chase after Him and He will wait
Then with a smile He will embrace you.
His true love is like no other
as hand-in-hand He leads you into your eternal life…

*¹⁰⁵ Your word is a lamp to my feet
And a light to my path.*

PSALM 119: 105

*⁵ Trust in the Lord with all your heart,
And lean not on your own understanding;
⁶ In all your ways acknowledge Him,
And He shall direct your paths.
⁷ Do not be wise in your own eyes;
Fear the Lord and depart from evil.
⁸ It will be health to your flesh,
And strength to your bones.*

PROVERBS 3: 5-8

*² He also brought me up out of a horrible pit,
Out of the miry clay,
And set my feet upon a rock,
And established my steps.*

PSALM 40: 2

Untitled XI

The Father

I never left you child
My heart and yours are linked
I know your future
Your past is past

Go where I lead you
There will be no signs
Just My words in your heart
Have no care for your future, child
My hand will guide you to where you belong
Lay your head at My feet at night
Know your dreams are with Me
I hold your precious heart close to My heart

The Child

I go where He leads me
No guides or maps do I need
His unspoken words lead me
Blind to the future
Filled with trust and His love
I know my feet shall land on solid ground
His guiding hand will lead me through the river of difficulty
I'll settle at His feet every night

Untitled XII

I kneel in front of You Father

My tears of thankfulness fall to the ground.

Thank you for my Life

Thank you for Your Love.

You guide my hand to create for You

Protect my mind from evil

Whisper to my spirit to inspire me.

Untitled XIII

Father God

Know that as I see people, so you shall

For I am there with them

Though they may never know until the end.

They will sense a peace and knowledge within you that they want a share of. Tell them they need only ask and I will give them their new life.

The peace I pour into this world

Grows and nurtures people who come to Me

Healing them from all the world's distresses.

⁷ and the peace of God, which surpasses all understanding, will guard your hearts and minds through Christ Jesus.
PHILIPPIANS 4: 7

Keep Asking, Seeking, Knocking

⁷ "Ask, and it will be given to you; seek, and you will find; knock, and it will be opened to you. ⁸ For everyone who asks receives, and he who seeks finds, and to him who knocks it will be opened."
MATTHEW 7: 7-8

The Good News of Salvation

*¹ "The Spirit of the Lord God is upon Me,
Because the Lord has anointed Me
To preach good tidings to the poor;
He has sent Me to heal the brokenhearted,
To proclaim liberty to the captives,
And the opening of the prison to those who are bound;
² To proclaim the acceptable year of the Lord,
And the day of vengeance of our God;
To comfort all who mourn,
³ To console those who mourn in Zion,
To give them beauty for ashes,
The oil of joy for mourning,
The garment of praise for the spirit of heaviness;
That they may be called trees of righteousness,
The planting of the Lord, that He may be glorified."*

Isaiah 61: 1-3

*⁶ Let the high praises of God be in their mouth,
And a two-edged sword in their hand,
⁷ To execute vengeance on the nations,
And punishments on the peoples;
⁸ To bind their kings with chains,
And their nobles with fetters of iron;*

Psalm 149: 6-8

Captured

I was a captive within an unseen prison. Its walls were invisible, yet I was held there – a prisoner.

For I knew not a way out – an escape – all remedies had been tried – I was weak, caught in the web that wrapped around me – not my body, although this showed the evidence of the web. No. It was my soul and spirit who were bound by the strands that were regularly dipped in a lotion of fear and all its fruit – anxiety, depression, apathy.

How did I survive? How did I not totally succumb? Was there an element of survival – a need to be free?

I had already broken free from the rusty chains that had imprisoned me in addiction, yet still my spirit knew I had not reached true freedom. More sickness, more inner pain – when would it all end?

It ended…

Jesus is my way, my truth and my life.

My Peaceful Healing Love

Broken. Shattered. Walls.

Healing. Loving. Hearts.

    Hands stretch out to one another

    Touching in their common entity

        No man will be alone

        No woman will ever mourn

            Their paths will lead to the one source

            They will rejoice in the purity of My love.

Crippled. Maimed. Healed.

Binding. Joining. Threads.

    Their entities are as one

    Knitted in the fabric of unity

        A tapestry of a landscape of lives

        Rich in the hues of My history

            Their hearts are open to My love

            They see only the beauty before them.

Fears shattered. Darkness revealed.

Roots of despair shrivel.

   Hopes are seeded

   The crop is bounteous

      The land of My beloved lies fertile before them

      Eyes are turned to Me

         My soft light bathes their wounds

         Rains wash away the dry dust of despair.

No ties. No boundaries.

Limitless love. Cherished hearts.

   Mountains will be conquered

   Oceans will be fathomed

      Let them come to Me to lay at My cross their bleeding hearts

      For freedom is the gift I give

         My sons and daughters will forever walk with Me

         Their dark pasts a dim reminder of what life was without

         My love.

[13] *I can do all things through Christ who strengthens me.*

PHILIPPIANS 4:13

Autumn is concealing but hinting at the harvest of healing that spring brings. Winter births the harvest that is hidden from sight. Spring is revealing the secrets that were hidden in the colours of Autumn and the Winter season. New life bursts forth to bring the Summer harvest.

A Season for Everything

A time for healing.
Furrows are ploughed
breaking through the soil's frosty skin
dross is extracted, cast aside
restoration awaits its call from spring.

A time for hope.
Spring is laced with anticipation
its sun melts and warms the soil's depths
seeds are sown into expectation
green buds jealously clasp their promises.

A time for restoration.
The harvest announces summer's arrival
the sweet warm mellowness of cut hay
seeps into the soul lying on its bed
satiating and inviting blissful sleep.

A time for reaping.
The harvest of healing is now gathered for prosperity
autumn's promises come to fruition
some are stored away for winter's hard times
others are relished and shared.

A time for healing…

The Rock

Fossil Beach held a special place in her heart. The girl would often go for walks there, along the track, with her Mum and Dad. All the way to the dead-end where craggy rocks stood as sentinels. Blocking any further exploration. An impasse. Her Mum was in her own world. Fleeting memories she would grasp on to so desperately. Always asking the same questions at the same place, along the track.

Yet, during all that time it was there. The rock – that large flat seat at the end of the track – it was always there. The girl just never saw who was sitting there. Waiting. For her.

She had sat there. On the day of one of their funerals – she couldn't remember which, the memories were all blurred into one. They had left within weeks of each other. The aloneness, the loss, the sadness all blended into the heavy winter sky suspended over the endless movement of the waves, rumbling rocks together in their dance. Was this what life was all about? The timeless rhythm of tides, waves and wind? Forever changing, beyond our control?

Unbeknownst to her, if she had reached out, He would have answered.

She can see now that what followed was a desperate attempt at keeping the pieces together. The already fractured history. But the glue was weak and bit by bit it all fell apart, dropping into the mire.

A fragile existence.

The truth – whatever that was.

The untruths – let's call it unspoken conspiracies – the hurt, the anger.

It all started to seep through the cracks. Patches of blood red. The clear water of tears (shed or unshed – let go or held in), more sickness, more fear (hidden or not), more anxiety and dark depression - all seeping through the cracks while the pressure within continued to build. Causing more and more fractures…

She tried so desperately to mend it. To plug it with a false happiness.

Familiar paths that no longer gave her the comfort she needed. Familiar doors that were locked, or opened to blank walls.

No entry...

Her options were narrowing, dragging her into a deep desperation...

Until that one particular day, of all those that had come to pass in her life, that one day, when the door that had long been closed, was flung wide open. And so their day of meeting came to pass.

Much healing.

Much prayer.

So much forgiveness.

And now she can stand on the rock. Hands outstretched. She meets Him who was always there. Waiting. For her. Waiting.

Her eternal Father. And she, a daughter.

That sacred place.

That rock.

Value

Man puts a monetary value on humans but God the Father values us, values me in a totally different way. I have value that exceeds this world.

Yes, I have accepted Jesus but I often struggle to LET Him truly love me. I have let men assign my value as easily as people around me did. Leaving me to measure myself next to others, and I found myself wanting because of the way other people behaved towards me. The scripture in Matthew 10: 29-31 tells how God cared about the birds and I am more valuable than the birds. Because God loved me, God had assigned me with value, not as my Aunts did. Not my family and not even myself, had given me the value Father God does.

Father God.

The same omnipotent God who spoke everything I have seen and heard into being, loved me, loves me. Even at my worst, when I sinned and fell away from the Lord, God loved me. He has taken care of me.

I am not perfect but Christ had valued me enough to die for me.

I have breathed in a peace, an assurance I have never known before. Men are not perfect. But my value didn't come from them. **It came from Jesus!!!**

And my identity does not come from man's opinion of me, but from my relationship with God the Father, God the Son and God the Holy Spirit.

²⁹ Are not two sparrows sold for a penny? Yet not one of them will fall to the ground outside your Father's care. ³⁰ And even the very hairs of your head are all numbered. ³¹ So don't be afraid; you are worth more than many sparrows. Matthew 10: 29-31 (NIV)

I love how this talks about God knowing us completely. This makes me feel safe and protected by the Father who created me. Whether you know Him or not, God loves you and He has already set up a way for you to know Him.

Meditate on Psalm 139 and see His love firsthand.

Untitled XIV

The curtains will be torn apart again

This time all sins will be exposed to the light

Those who wish to remain in sin will be condemned

Those who wish to reject sin will remain with Me

The condemned will be riven with absolute fear and terror, knowing they have reached the point of no return

Those who follow Me will be led to another place where great healing and much rejoicing will occur

They will be richly rewarded.

This is a warning to ALL sinners who reject Jesus.
Heaven and Eternity are the rewards of the Faithful.

Untitled XV

The golden thread weaves its way through the tapestry of life as a river roams across a landscape.

The golden thread is wound with many hues into a ball thrown into the universe to spin into eternity.

The golden thread is caught on the spirit, taking it with it as it journeys with its soul.

Spirit takes hold of its soul, to dance, swirling, twisting, in the atmosphere

Spinning as a cocoon is wound in the realm of the Holy Spirit.

The unity of the 3 threads - my spirit, my soul and the Holy Spirit

Entwined Supernaturally

Spinning

    with the Cross

        as He leads the dance

            across the Heavens.

Pathway of Promises

Father God

What is it child that brings you here to me?

The Child

I come for Your wisdom and to receive Your love.

Untitled XVI

To think, our little world is a mere speck in His universe, yet He knows and loves us all. I will never fathom His Love for me, I who was born imperfect but perfect in His eyes.

As I trod the Path towards Him with all its twists and turns, it was only He who knew that I would come to Him, broken, to be slowly healed by His loving balm.

How blessed I am!

1 O Lord, our Lord,
How excellent is Your name in all the earth,
Who have set Your glory above the heavens!
2 Out of the mouth of babes and nursing infants
You have ordained strength,
Because of Your enemies,
That You may silence the enemy and the avenger.
3 When I consider Your heavens, the work of Your fingers,
The moon and the stars, which You have ordained,
4 What is man that You are mindful of him,
And the son of man that You visit him?
5 For You have made him a little lower than the angels,
And You have crowned him with glory and honor.
6 You have made him to have dominion over the works of Your hands;
You have put all things under his feet,
7 All sheep and oxen -
Even the beasts of the field,
8 The birds of the air,
And the fish of the sea
That pass through the paths of the seas.
9 O Lord, our Lord,
How excellent is Your name in all the earth!

PSALM 8

Untitled XVII

Wait for that one second in time

                              There – it's gone!

Wait for that next heartbeat

                              There – it's gone!

Wait for that next heartbeat
Your heart beats in time
With the Father's heart

Drawing you closer…

> [6] *"… All flesh is grass,*
> *And all its loveliness is like the flower of the field.*
> [7] *The grass withers, the flower fades,*
> *Because the breath of the Lord blows upon it;*
> *Surely the people are grass.*
> [8] *The grass withers, the flower fades,*
> *But the word of our God stands forever."*
>
>   Isaiah 40: 6b – 8

Safety of Abiding in the Presence of God

¹ He who dwells in the secret place of the Most High
Shall abide under the shadow of the Almighty.
² I will say of the Lord, "He is my refuge and my fortress;
My God, in Him I will trust."
³ Surely He shall deliver you from the snare of the fowler
And from the perilous pestilence.
⁴ He shall cover you with His feathers,
And under His wings you shall take refuge;
His truth shall be your shield and buckler.

PSALM 91: 1-4

Jesus Gives True Rest

²⁸ Come to Me, all you who labor and are heavy laden, and I will give you rest. ²⁹ Take My yoke upon you and learn from Me, for I am gentle and lowly in heart, and you will find rest for your souls. ³⁰ For My yoke is easy and My burden is light."

MATTHEW 11: 28-30

¹⁷ Therefore, if anyone is in Christ, he is a new creation; old things have passed away; behold, all things have become new.

2 CORINTHIANS 5: 17

Untitled XVIII

The Father

Be still in Me

Know that I protect you

Listen to Me

Know that I will guide you.

Safe and secure in My arms

You will never be harmed

Where you go I will lead you

Know that My wing covers you.

Create for all the world to see

Believe in you as I believe in you.

Love you as I love you, My daughter

The precious one who came to Me in her troubles.

I healed you, I gave you a new life

I opened the door and closed many behind you

The changes I helped you make held no pain

As they had My hand on them.

Untitled XIX

Slowly, step by step, you flourished

And will continue until the end.

I will guide you to create for the world to see

My love for this world.

People will be touched and healed and will reach out for Me.

There is no fear in the life I gave you

There is no darkness in the light I gave you,

Stand in the shadow of My Cross

Wrap your arms around me

Feel My love.

---

[11] *For I know the thoughts that I think toward you, says the Lord, thoughts of peace and not of evil, to give you a future and a hope.*
JEREMIAH 29: 11

[7] *For God has not given us a spirit of fear, but of power and of love and of a sound mind.*
2 TIMOTHY 1: 7

Untitled XX

Travel through the desert, seeking out The Water

I will lead you to My Wells where you may slake your thirst and satisfy your hunger.

No bread, wine or meat can provide the same as this.

Others may search for the same satisfaction, but unless they know and love Me they will pass by My oases in blindness.

To know and love Me, is to see the world with different eyes – My eyes. For I remove the scales that blinded them, and I let My light shine in on their spirits.

The Promise of the Holy Spirit

[37] *On the last day, that great day of the feast, Jesus stood and cried out, saying, "If anyone thirsts, let him come to Me and drink.* [38] *He who believes in Me, as the Scripture has said, out of his heart will flow rivers of living water."*

JOHN 7: 37-38

Untitled XXI

He gave her eyes to see the world and read His Word

He gave her the sight to see into the Heavens

He gave her ears to hear the world and His Word and to hear His Voice

She was an empty chamber, unguarded and vulnerable, filled with darkness

Until His Spirit was given access.

He so filled the vacuum, nothing else could be present.

Presents for you

The Father

It said you are forever with Me. I have gifts for you that are priceless. Each one has a special meaning and use – each is unique. Angels will appear when you least expect them – some in human form - take great heed to what they say and do – this is the start of your new journey.

Angels will minister and guide you to do My work. You are so close to revelations – into realms and senses you have never experienced before. Take every one of My opportunities. You will know they are from Me. I will speak to you in different ways – remain aware and you will learn to recognise them. DO NOT be side-lined by what happens around you. Stay focused on Me and wait.

The Child

Thank You Father, that You love me so much. You keep giving so freely.

These words came to me after a vision I had one night of a hand offering me a piece of shining paper, but I couldn't read what was written on it.

Take note that the Angelic Host can only draw close to you as you speak and decree the Word of God over your life. Negative spoken words force the Angelic Host to withdraw from you.

Untitled XXII

Father God

I held you in My Hand

I breathed life into your spirit

I wrapped you in gifts

To be disclosed on your journey

I waited and watched as you grew.

The Child

I will wander no more

I will wonder in Him forever

God's Perfect Knowledge of Man

[14] *I will praise You, for I am fearfully and wonderfully made;*
Marvelous are Your works,
And that my soul knows very well.

PSALM 139: 14

Untitled XXIII

A life long lived is now nearing the end

A life full of ups and downs, joy and tragedy

A life that has touched others on its way through

A life that has left a mark… a legacy… a gift

A life so precious… so beautiful

A life long lived has ended now…

To where has it gone?

[51] Behold, I tell you a mystery: We shall not all sleep, but we shall all be changed— [52] in a moment, in the twinkling of an eye, at the last trumpet. For the trumpet will sound, and the dead will be raised incorruptible, and we shall be changed. [53] For this corruptible must put on incorruption, and this mortal must put on immortality. [54] So when this corruptible has put on incorruption, and this mortal has put on immortality, then shall be brought to pass the saying that is written: "Death is swallowed up in victory."
[55] "O Death, where is your sting?
O Hades, where is your victory?"
[56] The sting of death is sin, and the strength of sin is the law. [57] But thanks be to God, who gives us the victory through our Lord Jesus Christ.
[58] Therefore, my beloved brethren, be steadfast, immovable, always abounding in the work of the Lord, knowing that your labor is not in vain in the Lord.

1 CORINTHIANS 15: 51-58

Behind Closed Eyes

He waits to meet me there

I am not alone

I am with Him who shows me His infinite love

Emotions are drawn up from that bottomless well

Visions appear as parts of His messages

Colours float and merge

His words are heard not by my ears but by my spirit

My spirit speaks to the Holy Spirit interpreting our words.

Behind those eyes lies another realm for Him and me to meet.

Words are at times surplus as He speaks to my soul, calming, soothing.

12 For now we see in a mirror, dimly, but then face to face. Now I know in part, but then I shall know just as I also am known.
1 CORINTHIANS 13: 12

Untitled XXIV

A heart that holds no love for Me

Is like a hollow tree – empty of life

A heart that is replete with My Love

Is like a hallowed tree

Full of life eternal

Full of hope eternal

Untitled XXV

the wood has returned to the earth

the nails have rusted and broken down into the soil

dust to dust, ashes to ashes

This is not where His story is

His story lives on into eternity...

Our Final Victory

⁵¹ Behold, I tell you a mystery: We shall not all sleep, but we shall all be changed— ⁵² in a moment, in the twinkling of an eye, at the last trumpet. For the trumpet will sound, and the dead will be raised incorruptible, and we shall be changed. ⁵³ For this corruptible must put on incorruption, and this mortal must put on immortality. ⁵⁴ So when this corruptible has put on incorruption, and this mortal has put on immortality, then shall be brought to pass the saying that is written: "Death is swallowed up in victory."

1 CORINTHIANS 15: 51-54

Untitled XXVI

The Child

Where does the universe end Lord?

The Father

It does not – it is an element of time – My Time. Far beyond man's comprehension. They try to solve their questions with their theories – all as empty and pointless as a vacuum!!

Untitled XXVII

The wooden Cross was made by Me

For I created all things in this world

It is of Me, just as every thing is of Me

Everything has its purpose

Mankind may distort this for his own evil means

That is their choice – but they will pay the **ultimate price** for going against My purpose.

This is written in My Plan.

Those who make good use of what I provide will be rewarded

All things of Creation are there to glorify Me.

The Golden Harvest

the perfect circle

all encompassing

all surrounding

The Beauty of the relationship between a Spirit-filled Christian
and God the Father, God the Son and
God the Holy Spirit

¹⁴ *"... but whoever drinks of the water that I shall give him will never thirst. But the water that I shall give him will become in him a fountain of water springing up into everlasting life."*

                 JOHN 4: 14

The True Vine

¹ *"I am the true vine, and My Father is the vinedresser. ² Every branch in Me that does not bear fruit He takes away; and every branch that bears fruit He prunes, that it may bear more fruit."*

                 JOHN 15: 1-2

The Harvest

The wind is My carrier, blowing My seeds far and wide across the globe.

My plan is for the seeds to land where they are needed, where they will grow and nurture others in My Gardens of Faith, Hope and Glory.

None will lay on barren soil or rocks as they will obey My commands for where to go.

My water will quench their thirsts and My soil will provide all the nourishment they require.

From seeds to plants they grow, some flowering and spreading their fruit.

Others are there to be pruned, their cuttings to be transplanted elsewhere.

Those that grow to massive trees provide shade and protection from the travesties of this world.

My Son will always warm them, even in the darkest, dankest places.

All they know they need to do is to open their hearts, where their spirits dwell and My warmth and love will come forth to all those who thirst.

Go forth in the wind. Close your eyes and listen to My Voice.

Untitled XXVIII

The Father

I will fill your blank page

I will cover your blank canvas

With the colours of My Creation

from My Rainbow Palette.

Untitled XXIX

He made a minute mark on the canvas

By adding lines, shapes and forms, the mark slowly grew

Lights and darks gave depth and a hint of what was to be

Transformed gradually

Content with what He had created, He smiled

Yet while it was still so small He passed it

To the bearer to love and care for.

He watched over His creation as she grew, stumbling at first

He gave her strength to move forward on the path He set before her.

The Creative Child

pots of colours for the senses felt

pens with words to say how it felt

        stir the two together, turn it upside down

            spilling across the floor

rubbing my hands in the rainbow lexicon

            let the wind dry the canvas

let the letters meet together

      then, and only then, turn the light on

        for this is for the world to see

how He offered His hand to me:

    the creation walking with her Creator.

Splinters of the Cross

I created the trees that made My Cross.

Splinters, stained with My blood, were left to decay,

returning to the earth.

Picked up as dust by the wind,

My blood was carried

across the world to be laid to rest.

Spiritually, the dust with My Blood

ascended into the atmosphere to land in

My Chosen Ones' hearts.

Divine Purpose

the spirit flows as the blood that courses through the veins

the soul floats anchored in the vessel

spirits await the invitation to meet His Spirit

some may never encounter Him, the privilege is not taken

others know their appointed time will come

when the soul asks for the invitation

for it knows that when He joined them

the soul and the spirit

that divine partnership

their destiny was to know Him

their purpose was His Purpose

15 *My frame was not hidden from You,*

When I was made in secret,

And skillfully wrought in the lowest parts of the earth.

16 *Your eyes saw my substance, being yet unformed.*

And in Your book they all were written,

The days fashioned for me,

When as yet there were none of them.

PSALM 139: 15-16

Love Letter to Jesus

I gave my old toxic life to You Lord.

In return You gave me the freedom I needed to fly on Your wings. I've explored the world, led by You, to places You wanted me to be. I've discovered the Well of Creativity that I could never reach for all those years.

Every stumbling step I took, every tear I spent, were all recorded… right to the moment that I gave my life to You. And so I travel on this journey knowing that not only will You be with me for every heartbeat, every breath, You will be there to greet me for my next journey.

You knew me as You created me. You have known me from the beginning of time.

Thank you Jesus with all my heart.

Jesus Gives True Rest

²⁸ *"Come to Me, all you who labor and are heavy laden, and I will give you rest.* ²⁹ *Take My yoke upon you and learn from Me, for I am gentle and lowly in heart, and you will find rest for your souls.* ³⁰ *For My yoke is easy and My burden is light."*

MATTHEW 11: 28-30

Ffald y Brenin, Wales I

From my room looking at the Cross and listening to music.
I watched as a bird landed on the Cross.

Let all of My Creation alight on My Cross

For I will bear all who come to Me

With their troubles and sorrows

I carry the weight of the world

Their footsteps tread the path to Me

Heavy with their burdens and woes

To pause for a time, to share with Me what I already know

I open My Heart to them and beseech them to lay

their load at My Cross

For this is the only way to lighten their burdens

It was through My spilt blood that they were given the freedom to approach Me

Full of awe and love, they lay their sins and sadness at My feet.

Ffald y Brenin, Wales II

Hard sharp stones finally offer me a place to sit

my comfort comes from leaning into the yielding wood of

Your Cross

birds soar above

 dancing in Your freedom

singing Your praises

sweet grassy perfumes drift in the breeze across the valley

 as the sun plays with the sky

my peace is in Your silence as You speak of Your love for me

and for this world.

The Truth Shall Make You Free

36 Therefore if the Son makes you free, you shall be free indeed.
                                                                    JOHN 8: 36

Masquerade

this face she wears for this friend

                                        this face she wears for that friend

this face she wears to work

                                        this face she wears for the photo

this face she wears for her family

                                        this face she wears for her lover.

                  Only the Father sees her heart.

[7] *But the Lord said to Samuel, "Do not look at his appearance or at his physical stature, because I have refused him. For the Lord does not see as man sees; for man looks at the outward appearance, but the Lord looks at the heart."*

                                                      1 SAMUEL 16: 7

The Door

The mute heart

the deaf soul

the blind spirit

    know not where the door is

        stumbling, crawling through the darkness

            the precipice approaches…

            Till just before the final fatal step

        the earth shudders

      lightning flashes in their eyes

    and turning

the Open Door is revealed.

Keep Asking, Seeking, Knocking

⁷ "Ask, and it will be given to you; seek, and you will find; knock, and it will be opened to you. ⁸ For everyone who asks receives, and he who seeks finds, and to him who knocks it will be opened."
                                                          MATTHEW 7: 7-8

¹⁸ "Assuredly, I say to you, whatever you bind on earth will be bound in heaven, and whatever you loose on earth will be loosed in heaven.
¹⁹ "Again I say to you that if two of you agree on earth concerning anything that they ask, it will be done for them by My Father in heaven. ²⁰ For where two or three are gathered together in My name, I am there in the midst of them."

MATTHEW 18: 18-20

¹⁹ "And I will give you the keys of the kingdom of heaven, and whatever you bind on earth will be bound in heaven, and whatever you loose on earth will be loosed in heaven."

MATTHEW 16: 19

The Well

Your shadow of light covered me

as I reached out from my darkness

You showed me where my heart lay waiting

at the bottom of that well.

Deep crimson, nestled in purple velvet

a silver key lay across it

You took my hand and together we reached down...

We unlocked my heart...

This poem speaks of the Keys of the Kingdom, the secrets of the Father's heart that He only releases as we seek His face. The Keys on one hand open the secrets of the Father's heart to us and on the other hand are weapons to pull down the power of Satan's kingdom.
The Keys open up the Word of God so we understand how to implement it.

Untitled XXX

Somewhere in a dream she passed the bloodline jewel to me and hid it in the well for me to find. Deep crimson, heart-shaped, it was nestled in purple velvet.

In loving gratitude to my great grandmother Mary Amelia Hebblewhite.

What a gift you gave to me!

If only I could fully realise it, Lord.

This speaks about recognising the Godly inheritance of receiving Redemption through the blood of Jesus as we accept Him as our Saviour.

Untitled XXXI

The Child

I hear Your voice in my spirit

Your words are carried in the wind of my soul

I reach out and catch them as they alight on my mind

They drift down into my heart, settling in my soul.

Oh Lord, You have so much You want to tell me and I have so much I want to know of You.

Lead me into the Chambers where we speak.

Where is my spirit?

Father God

Your spirit resides in your heart and reveals itself in your eyes. It shimmers in its energy.

It was the first thing I created of you – The Seed. I built the framework of your character around it. My Holy Spirit lives within you.

The Anointing at Bethany

1 Then, six days before the Passover, Jesus came to Bethany, where Lazarus was who had been dead, whom He had raised from the dead. *2* There they made Him a supper; and Martha served, but Lazarus was one of those who sat at the table with Him. *3* Then Mary took a pound of very costly oil of spikenard, anointed the feet of Jesus, and wiped His feet with her hair. And the house was filled with the fragrance of the oil.
4 But one of His disciples, Judas Iscariot, Simon's son, who would betray Him, said, *5* "Why was this fragrant oil not sold for three hundred denarii and given to the poor?" *6* This he said, not that he cared for the poor, but because he was a thief, and had the money box; and he used to take what was put in it.
7 But Jesus said, "Let her alone; she has kept this for the day of My burial. *8* For the poor you have with you always, but Me you do not have always."

JOHN 12: 1-8

The Redeemer of Israel

1 But now, thus says the LORD, who created you, O Jacob,
And He who formed you, O Israel:
"Fear not, for I have redeemed you;
I have called you by your name;
You are Mine."

ISAIAH 43: 1

The Seed

She passes silently in the night.

The wind whispers His message – "Go!"

Through the cracks of time, of eternity

To where her life began.

This was where the seed was planted.

This was where He etched her soul.

The night holds all secrets.

Faltering, she grasps the seed.

Not daring to look up, she kisses His feet

Her tears wash over His toes.

How could she have ever denied Him?

The essence of love sweetens her plea for forgiveness.

His unspoken words reassure her.

He hears, He sees, He watches, He listens.

All of mankind can be seen from His seat.

He sees not just them, but the fears that dwell in their hearts

The fears that stained their pure souls after their birth

Fears that can only be washed away by His blood.

¹¹ *If I say, "Surely the darkness shall fall on me,"*
Even the night shall be light about me;
¹² *Indeed, the darkness shall not hide from You,*
But the night shines as the day;
The darkness and the light are both alike to You.

PSALM 139: 11-12

⁸ *But now, O Lord,*
You are our Father;
We are the clay, and You our potter;
And all we are the work of Your hand.

ISAIAH 64:8

Untitled XXXII

Father God

Meet Me where the spirits run like streams across the arid desert

Meeting at My oasis where Life and Love flourish

My Spirit shifts as a cloud, softly guided by

My Breeze that moves with My Hand

The Child

Swirling like Water, He flows into the cracks

making His way through chasms of the mind

His touch is barely felt, a feather against skin

Let your spirit flow towards Him and embrace when they meet

Untitled XXXIII

Hark! She awakens in her soul! The seed has brought forth its shoot – the growth has begun. Upwards to Heaven it will grow with branches spreading across the world. Blossoms will paint the sky, drifting to earth, fruit will follow – enough for anyone who chooses to see and hear My messages of the love I have for this world.

The True Vine

[1] "I am the true vine, and My Father is the vinedresser. [2] Every branch in Me that does not bear fruit He takes away; and every branch that bears fruit He prunes, that it may bear more fruit."

JOHN 15: 1-2

The Way of the Righteous and the End of the Ungodly

[1] Blessed is the man
Who walks not in the counsel of the ungodly,
Nor stands in the path of sinners,
Nor sits in the seat of the scornful;
[2] But his delight is in the law of the Lord,
And in His law he meditates day and night.
[3] He shall be like a tree
Planted by the rivers of water,
That brings forth its fruit in its season,
Whose leaf also shall not wither;
And whatever he does shall prosper.

PSALM 1: 1-3

Untitled XXXIV

Festooned among the litter are the letters of the law as it was

My Words are now held closely to the hearts of the ones who have found Me

Those who love and adore Me.

Not only that, they have learned to listen to My Voice

As it speaks softly into their spirits.

As they listen, they learn of My Ways, My Teaching as they have never been heard before

For they are Words especially crafted for their spirits to hear.

Unique letters forming unique Words in a unique language that is only for the listener to understand.

If another spirit were to hear them they would make no sense.

So I speak these Words into you, knowing there is a place within you that accepts and understands.

Absorb them and let them soak into you for they are the lifeblood of your identity.

Do not try to translate or analyse, just be still and allow your senses to absorb the meanings.

⁸But now, O Lord,
You are our Father;
We are the clay, and You our potter;
And all we are the work of Your hand.

ISAIAH 64: 8

The Master's Hand

God reminded me that He is a God of restoration. As I pondered on this, He brought to mind a picture of a furniture restorer.
An old side table with one drawer, a broken leg, covered in layers and layers of crud and build up from the environment and many hands that have touched it, sits left alone.

A craftsman views the broken piece with love as he sees the beauty within. He then goes about his work removing the years of build-up, slowly sanding everything back very carefully so as not to damage what is underneath.

Sometimes he has to rub a bit harder, but he knows how far to rub without damaging the hidden gem and beauty within.
He puts the broken parts back on then starts to rub and polish the areas where he has removed the crud. He rubs with tenderness and love taking his time to make sure he fills all the gaps while rubbing all the good oil back in to restore its beauty.

The craftsman lovingly looks on his work as he restores it to how it was originally made.
When people look at a piece a craftsman has made, they are amazed at how such beauty is created.

Our God, the Master Craftsman, looks at each of us lovingly as He restores us to how we were originally made so that when complete we can the show the beauty of the Creator.
May the Lord our Creator continue to rub and polish each one of us so that we can bring Him glory in all we do and then shine for the world to see our amazing God.

In Tune with The Father

Dear Father thank You for bringing me here

Thank You for my gift of creativity, of creating for You

You gave me my life, my soul, my journey, my path

I will follow You wherever You lead me.

To be here in Your Holy Spirit is to be in Your grace

My life is Yours to mould, to chisel, to fashion as You will

I surrender to Your guidance, to learn and give to the world

Whatever is in Your plan, I will live my life for.

My eyes are Your eyes, my mind is Your mind

My hands will do as You wish

I know whatever You have me do will never be impossible

For all is possible when I breathe with You.

The King of Glory and His Kingdom

1 The earth is the Lord's, and all its fullness,
The world and those who dwell therein.
2 For He has founded it upon the seas,
And established it upon the waters.
3 Who may ascend into the hill of the Lord?
Or who may stand in His holy place?

⁴ *He who has clean hands and a pure heart,*
Who has not lifted up his soul to an idol,
Nor sworn deceitfully.
⁵ *He shall receive blessing from the Lord,*
And righteousness from the God of his salvation.
⁶ *This is Jacob, the generation of those who seek Him,*
Who seek Your face.

PSALM 24: 1-6

¹⁴ *"Because he has set his love upon Me, therefore I will deliver him;*
I will set him on high, because he has known My name.
¹⁵ *He shall call upon Me, and I will answer him;*
I will be with him in trouble;
I will deliver him and honor him.
¹⁶ *With long life I will satisfy him,*
And show him My salvation."

PSALM 91: 14-16

⁵ *Trust in the* LORD *with all your heart,*
And lean not on your own understanding;
⁶ *In all your ways acknowledge Him,*
And He shall direct your paths.

PROVERBS 3: 5-6

¹³ *I can do all things through Christ who strengthens me.*

PHILIPPIANS 4: 13

⁹ *And He said to me, "My grace is sufficient for you, for My strength is made perfect in weakness." Therefore most gladly I will rather boast in my infirmities, that the power of Christ may rest upon me.*

2 CORINTHIANS 12: 9

Untitled XXXV

Her hand writes of My Love

Her eyes see the Words as they appear

Her senses describe what is around her

His hand writes of life as it is in this world and elsewhere

See the Words flow out on to the page

Now anyone can read them and take from them what they wish

Love is a wordless language spoken by all tongues

Too often false words of love are spoken

They fall as barbs on the heart, to fester into hate

True love need not be uttered

For it is there to be heard by the senses and the spirit.

The Scribe writes of life as it is on this earth and the heavens

Her pen is guided by Me as My Words flow out onto the page

My Messages are there for the world to read

Each letter is formed into a Word reaching out

To be seen by eyes that yearn for a faultless Love

A Love that has no limits and exists for all time

My Love touches the senses and the spirit

This is My Love

Open your heart and allow your spirit to read not just these Words

But to embrace the Love contained in them

Allow them to wash away your tears and pain

You ask yourself – How could such a Love exist?

I wait for your question

Your heart will reach out and My answer will be given to you.

Untitled XXXVI

The rhythm of life is complex.

Each beat creates an energy that is absorbed

whether it be animal, plant, water, oxygen, a grain of sand.

Every sound continues to reverberate through space, to be heard into eternity.

The Child

How can I describe you God, my Father? I can only describe You with the word Love – a Love that is beyond the dimensions of this world. No-one will ever truly understand the completeness of Your Love until their time comes to finally be with You.

You cannot be described physically as we cannot comprehend Your vastness, Your power, Your strength and… Your Love.

The Saviour, Jesus Christ

If I poured out all My tears till My blood ran, it would not be enough to describe My Love.

Untitled XXXVII

This land has no boundaries, no territories

All is in harmony, peace, synchronicity

Time does not exist

Space moves with space

All spirits praise Me in endless love

Angels' voices sing of My Glory, endlessly

Peace flows in the rivers and the wind

Nothing is tainted, purity is the essence

All beings are in their perfect state

Restored to how they were meant to be

Their souls are rested, their spirits are harmonious

At peace with themselves and others

All their questions are answered by Me

When they enter into the glory of My Presence

Scribe of Life

Father God

Pick up My Pen and record My Words.

I love this World, if only they all realised.

One day each one will be given the choice:

Me or nothing – not one thing to hold on to

For all "things" will fall away – except My Love.

Here lies their choice: Me and all I encompass or nothing.

All things they cherish and are slaves to will disappear

They will realise it was all of no value

Yet if they had come to Me they would have been provided for.

The true value lies within Me.

*²³ Search me, O God, and know my heart;
Try me, and know my anxieties;
²⁴ And see if there is any wicked way in me,
And lead me in the way everlasting.*

PSALM 139: 23-24

*¹⁷ No weapon formed against you shall prosper,
And every tongue which rises against you in judgment
You shall condemn.
This is the heritage of the servants of the Lord,
And their righteousness is from Me,"
Says the Lord.*

ISAIAH 54: 17

⁶ Be strong and of good courage, for to this people you shall divide as an inheritance the land which I swore to their fathers to give them. ⁷ Only be strong and very courageous, that you may observe to do according to all the law which Moses My servant commanded you; do not turn from it to the right hand or to the left, that you may prosper wherever you go. ⁸ This Book of the Law shall not depart from your mouth, but you shall meditate in it day and night, that you may observe to do according to all that is written in it. For then you will make your way prosperous, and then you will have good success. ⁹ Have I not commanded you? Be strong and of good courage; do not be afraid, nor be dismayed, for the Lord your God is with you wherever you go."

JOSHUA 1: 6-9

The Song of the Warrior

Thank you Jesus that I am yours
And You are mine.

All that I have, I offer up to You,
All that You are I receive, even into my DNA.

I acknowledge that my level of peace and joy,
In all circumstances,
Is a measuring stick of my yieldedness to You.

I declare that with You, I am fearless and courageous.
I carry the resurrection power of the Holy Spirit that raised you,
Jesus, from the grave.

No weapon formed against me shall prosper,
Nothing can separate me from Your love, Your presence and Your provision.

Help me to carry my daily sacrifices with love, grace and mercy.
They pave the way for me to carry your Glory and Power, to bring Heaven to Earth.

Today I dedicate my extraordinary life to You afresh,
I love you Jesus.
Have your way Lord.

The Timeless One

An unknown language speaks to you

You do not recognise the words

Yet you know the meaning

That rests in your heart calling

For only you to hear

To know The Truth

The Mist swirls in the desert dunes of your soul

Alighting on the innermost you

Seeking out questions that are yet to be asked

Questions answered from The Knowledge unknown to man

From the outermost stars to the grains of sand in the desert

All connected, drawn together in a common history

All born from The One Source, The One Creator whose time has no limits

As rocks turn to sand, so the sand is returned to rocks in an endless cycle

Seconds are years, millennia are days

Each creation returns to its Creator, The Timeless One

The 3

Christ is The Structure

Holy Spirit is The Glue

I AM The Creator.

Father God / Creator

Live each moment knowing that I AM with you.

> ^{23} *Search me, O God, and know my heart...*
> ^{24} *...And lead me in the way everlasting.*
>
> **PSALM 139: 23A & 24B**

*¹³ For You formed my inward parts;
You covered me in my mother's womb.
¹⁴ I will praise You, for I am fearfully and wonderfully made;
Marvelous are Your works,
And that my soul knows very well.
¹⁵ My frame was not hidden from You,
When I was made in secret,
And skillfully wrought in the lowest parts of the earth.
¹⁶ Your eyes saw my substance, being yet unformed.
And in Your book they all were written,
The days fashioned for me,
When as yet there were none of them.*

PSALM 139: 13-16

Acknowledgements

I give my heartfelt thanks and gratitude to the two people who have also contributed to this work and who assisted and encouraged me during its creation.

To my family and friends who also encouraged me and listened to my updates of the progress of this book or who have just been there for me and loved me, thank you.

To my dear friend who became my very patient art teacher, while at the same time introducing me to the Holy Spirit and all His Creativity – God bless you! Thank you for your invaluable guidance.

I will eternally thank the two servants of God who were obedient to Him and were there to guide me during that very special time as I gave my life to Christ, and while He healed me.

And I also want to show my gratitude to my great grandmother Mary Amelia Hebblewhite (nee Busby). I never knew you, yet I know now just how special you were and are to God. You were taught to listen to your Saviour's voice from when you were a young girl. You heard it and obeyed.

Above all, to Father God, Jesus Christ, and my Comforter and Source of Inspiration the Holy Spirit, I thank You for my life.

H †

The Scribe of Life

I am a child of God who brought me into this world for His purpose.

P.S. If you have ever wondered if God has a sense of humour – consider the platypus!

About the authors

Helen Bishop, the main contributor to this book, gave her life to Jesus Christ in 2010. She had been ill for some time and had sought various treatments to no avail. It was not until God opened the door to His true inner healing, which she so desperately needed, that she began to heal spiritually and physically.

Since then, He has revealed to her the "well of creativity" that she always knew was there but could not access. She began to create under the guidance of the Holy Spirit who would, and continues to, give her pictures and instructions on what to create, and words to write.

Just as happened to Helen, Jesus came and lifted the three other contributors of this book out of the mirey clay and set their feet upon the rock, to walk into freedom and victory. And in that freedom, He has blessed them to be more in the Kingdom of God than they ever dreamed they could be.

1 I waited patiently for the Lord;
And He inclined to me,
And heard my cry.
2 He also brought me up out of a horrible pit,
Out of the miry clay,
And set my feet upon a rock,
And established my steps.
3 He has put a new song in my mouth
Praise to our God;
Many will see it and fear,
And will trust in the Lord.

PSALM 40: 1-3

www.ingramcontent.com/pod-product-compliance
Lightning Source LLC
Chambersburg PA
CBHW070308010526
44107CB00056B/2529